COSICH

Spartacus

Russell Punter

Illustrated by Gustavo Mazali

Reading consultant: Alison Kelly
University of Roehampton

The people in this story

Here are some of the people you will read about in this book. They all lived in Italy around 2,000 years ago.

Spartacus - the leader of an army of rebel slaves.

Lentulus Batiatus - the owner of a school for gladiators.

Crixus - a Celtic slave. Spartacus' co-leader.

Caius Claudius Glaber - a Roman officer sent to recapture the rebels on Vesuvius, a dormant volcano.

Gnaeus Clodianus - a Roman officer sent to attack the rebels on the Adriatic coast.

Lucius Gellius Publicola - a Roman officer sent to attack the rebels on the Adriatic coast.

Marcus Licinius Crassus - the richest man in Rome. Spartacus' arch enemy.

Mummius - a Roman officer under Crassus who attacked the rebels at Ancona.

Pompey - a Roman general, known as 'Pompey the Great', sent to help defeat the rebels in southern Italy.

Spartacus' journey

Spartacus journeyed all over Italy. This map shows his route from Naples, where he started out in 73 B.C., to his last battle in 71 B.C. by the River Silarus.

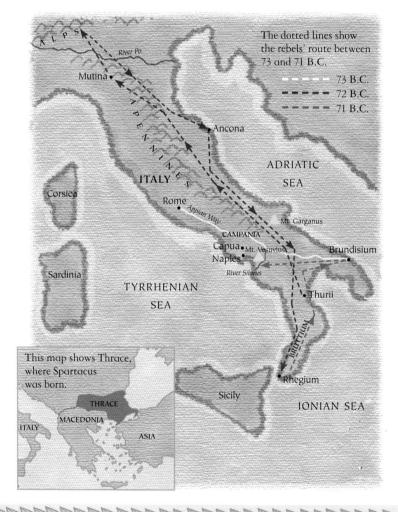

The dotted lines show the rebels' route between 73 and 71 B.C.

— — —	73 B.C.
— — —	72 B.C.
— — —	71 B.C.

ALPS

River Po

Mutina

APENNINES

Ancona

ITALY

Corsica

Rome

Appian Way

ADRIATIC SEA

Mt. Garganus

CAMPANIA

Capua • Mt. Vesuvius

Naples

River Silarus

Brundisium

Sardinia

TYRRHENIAN SEA

Thurii

BRUTTIUM

Rhegium

Sicily

IONIAN SEA

This map shows Thrace, where Spartacus was born.

THRACE

MACEDONIA

ITALY

ASIA

Contents

Chapter 1

Sold into slavery

Spartacus was marched through the Roman slave market, the rough ropes on his arms cutting into his skin.

It was a sweltering summer's day, just over two thousand years ago.

Spartacus had been brought to the market in Naples by a Roman soldier named Quintus.

Removing the ropes, Quintus shoved his prisoner before a sly-looking man.

"Well Lentulus Batiatus," said Quintus, "What do you think?"

"Hmm, not bad," said Batiatus.

"This coward deserted from my legion," sneered Quintus.

"I'm no coward," growled
Spartacus, raising his fists in anger.

I'm not
afraid to
fight!

"He has spirit," Batiatus laughed,
"and muscles. Shame he betrayed us
and he's no longer a soldier. But he'll
make a good gladiator. I'll take him."

Spartacus was thrown into a cart.
It was full of men captured by the
Romans from across their republic.

"Welcome aboard, friend," said one. "The name's Crixus."

Spartacus recognized the accent. "A Celt, right?" he asked. The burly man nodded.

"I'm from Thrace," Spartacus said proudly. "And if I hadn't joined the Roman army, I'd be there now. Where are we going?"

"To be trained as gladiators at Batiatus' school in Capua."

"We'll still be slaves," scowled Spartacus, "Just like millions of others, working for nothing for rich Romans."

As the cart rattled off through the countryside, Spartacus seethed with anger. He had been born free. Whatever it took, he was determined to be free once more.

9

Chapter 2

Escape

Life at Batiatus' gladiator school was tough. If Spartacus or the others did anything wrong, they were punished with whips and swords.

At first, the slaves used wooden weapons against dummies. But soon they had to fight each other. Spartacus often found himself trading blows with men who had become good friends.

At night, they slept in small, dark cells, constantly under guard.

"We have to get out of here," whispered Spartacus to Crixus, as they were marched to their cells one night. "Will you help me?"

"Of course," replied Crixus. "But how? We'll need weapons. The wooden swords we use for training would be useless."

"I have an idea," said Spartacus.

In the days that followed, Spartacus took every opportunity to whisper the details of his daring plan to the rest of the gladiators.

As they were marching from the cells one morning, Spartacus gave a signal.

A group of gladiators charged into the guards, sending them crashing to the ground.

Spartacus led the gladiators down the narrow corridors until they came to the kitchen.

Horrified cooks fled in terror as the rebels grabbed hefty choppers and skewers.

Armed with their makeshift weapons, the gladiators fought their way out of the school.

In the street outside, Spartacus noticed two wagons. They were piled high with equipment and clothes used in the gladiator fights at the nearby arena.

"Real weapons! Take all you can, men," Spartacus cried, and the gladiators eagerly grabbed swords, spears, helmets, tunics and shields.

Led by Spartacus, the mob of men stormed out of town. They headed into the countryside, plundering supplies as they went.

"Now we need a safe camp to plan our next move," panted Spartacus. His eye rested on a far-off mountain. "Where better than Vesuvius?"

Chapter 3

Volcano

Although Vesuvius was a massive volcano, it hadn't erupted for years. For now, all the gladiators had to worry about was the climb ahead.

On the side of the volcano, the rebels rested, sharing out the plundered food and drink. Then they elected leaders, including Spartacus and Crixus.

News of their escape spread throughout Capua, and they were joined by runaway slaves, including many women and children, from nearby farms.

The frustrated Capuans sent local soldiers to deal with the rebels. But Spartacus' men quickly defeated them.

Soon, word of Spartacus and the others reached Rome. The city was home to the senators who controlled the Roman republic.

All their best legions were fighting abroad. So a group of semi-trained soldiers, under the command of Claudius Glaber, was sent to defeat Spartacus. They set up camp near the top of Vesuvius, trapping the rebels at the summit.

"What do we do now?" Crixus asked Spartacus. "The only other way down is a sheer drop."

Spartacus looked around the mountainside for inspiration. All he could see were the tangled vines that covered the landscape.

"Got it!" he exclaimed. "If we pull up these vines, we can knot them together and use them to climb down."

The rebels waited until
dark. Then they silently
descended the side of the
volcano until they
reached a ledge.
"Follow me!"
whispered Spartacus,
leading his allies
around the
mountain.

Up ahead, he spotted the Roman
camp. "Let's surprise our enemies."
The rebels charged out of
the gloom and leaped on the
unsuspecting Romans.

Panicked, Claudius and his men
fled down the volcano in terror.
"Look at them run," laughed
Spartacus. "We're unbeatable."

As winter approached, another officer and his men were sent from Rome. But they were humiliated and defeated too.

Spartacus reckoned his rebel army was now at least 70,000 strong.

They had made camps throughout Campania in southern Italy, raiding local towns for supplies. It seemed as if no one could stop them.

Chapter 4

Triumph and tragedy

Spartacus decided to spend the winter months in the rebel camp at Thurii, where he used his knowledge of Roman battle techniques to train new recruits.

As spring arrived, the rebels'
leaders gathered to decide their
next move.

"I say we cross the Apennine
Mountains, then march north to
the Alps," said Spartacus. "From
there, we can all return to the
freedom of our homelands."

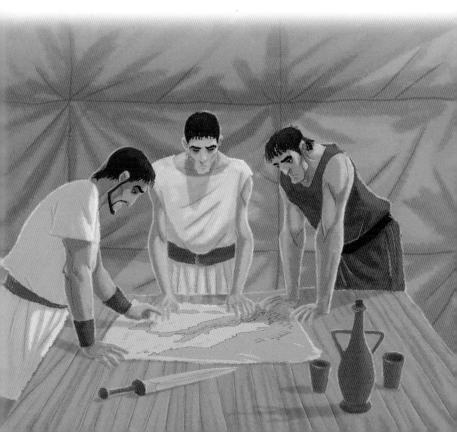

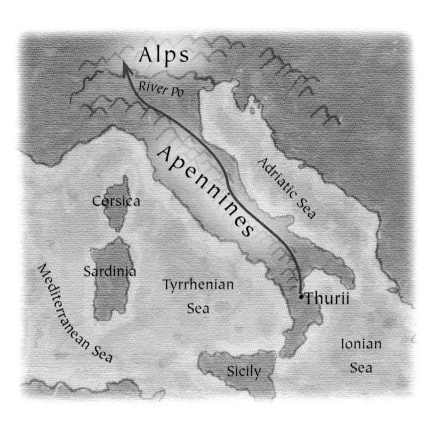

But Crixus looked uneasy. "I'd rather take my chances here," he said. "We've become so strong, we could live well, if we stay alert."

Spartacus would miss his friend, but he decided to move on without Crixus and his fellow Celts.

Spartacus and the remaining rebels began their long march across the Apennines. To begin with, the steep slopes were rugged and dusty. Progress was slow and hard. It was only as they moved north, that the landscape started to become greener.

When they approached the
Adriatic coast, the rebels had a
shock. A Roman legion, led by
Gnaeus Clodianus, was lying
in wait.

Spartacus had lost none of his
fighting spirit. "We'll attack them
head on," he ordered.

The rebel army charged into the wall of Romans. The battle was a hard one, but eventually Spartacus and his men were victorious.

They didn't have long to re-group.

A scout rushed up to Spartacus, "There's another legion right behind us," he gasped, "commanded by Lucius Gellius Publicola."

Spartacus ordered his men to turn and attack the approaching forces. Once again, the former slaves proved to be the better fighters, capturing hundreds more Romans.

Battered and confused, the remains of Clodianus' and Publicola's legions retreated to Rome.

Spartacus ordered all the Roman prisoners to be killed, before heading north once more.

Then a messenger brought terrible news. Before he'd caught up with Spartacus, Publicola had attacked Crixus and his army.

Two thousand rebels had been killed, including Crixus himself.

As he marched towards the Alps, Spartacus vowed to avenge his friend's death.

Chapter 5

A change of plan

As the towering Alps came into view, Spartacus and his followers approached the town of Mutina.

"Not much further now," cried Spartacus enthusiastically. At that moment, a group of Romans broke cover and attacked.

This was the army of the local governor. But they were no match for Spartacus' band of tough, battle-scarred fighters.

"Now I can take my revenge
for the death of Crixus," thought
Spartacus.

When the Romans had been
defeated, he had the survivors
divided into pairs and given swords.

"I command you to fight to the
death, like gladiators!" he cried.

The Romans had no choice but to obey. A bloody contest followed.

When the gruesome spectacle was over, Spartacus and his followers marched on, to the foothills of the Alps.

"Across there lies a new life," declared Spartacus. "Go back to your countries as free men and women, not slaves."

A few of the rebels said farewell to their comrades and headed up into the mountains.

But, to his surprise, Spartacus found that most of his followers didn't want to go.

"Let's stay in Italy and take what we want from the Romans," said one.

"They'll never be able to make us slaves again," added another.

Spartacus thought long and
hard. Perhaps his allies were right.
"Very well," he said at last. "We
shall live as warriors. Let the
Romans try to stop us if they dare."

Chapter 6

A deadly enemy

Meanwhile, in Rome, the senators were becoming more and more frustrated by Spartacus.

"There must be someone who can deal with this upstart," moaned one.

"I've asked for volunteers," said another. "But so far, no one has..."

"I hear you need help," a gruff voice interrupted. The senators turned to see Marcus Licinius Crassus, the richest man in Rome.

"Can you defeat this common gladiator?" asked a senator.

"With the right men," replied Crassus coolly. He may have been wealthy, but he wanted glory too.

"We can spare you ten legions," said the senator. "That's fifty thousand trained soldiers."

Crassus smirked. "Then Spartacus is as good as dead."

By now, Spartacus had headed south, to a place named Ancona. Crassus set off in pursuit.

On the way, he sent a message to Mummius, the commander of two legions near Spartacus' camp.

"Tell him to steer his men behind Spartacus," he told the messenger, "But not to attack until I say so."

Yes, sir.

Mummius, however, was eager
to finish off Spartacus himself.
Ignoring Crassus, his legions
engaged the rebels in battle.

Mummius was defeated – and
worse was to come. As punishment
for disobeying him, Crassus decided
that the surviving troops should
be decimated.

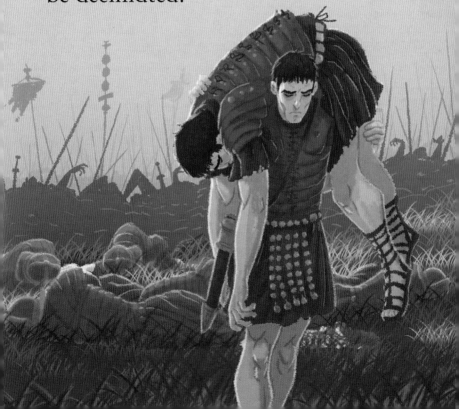

All the soldiers were divided
into groups of ten and made to
draw lots. The unlucky man in each
group who picked the black stone
from a bag of white ones was killed.

Having shown his own troops
who was boss, Crassus turned his
attention to Spartacus.

For the first time, Spartacus found himself up against an enemy as strong as he was. Crassus won battle after battle. The rebels were forced to Bruttium at the southern tip of Italy.

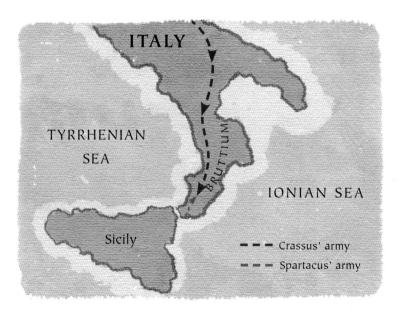

"We must have reinforcements," decided a weary Spartacus. "And I think I know where to find them..."

Chapter 7

Plotting with pirates

Spartacus sat outside a rough dockside tavern. The place was full of pirates who plundered Roman ships across the Mediterranean.

"So we have a deal, then?" said Spartacus, handing over a bag of coins to two tough-looking pirates. "You'll take two thousand of us across to Sicily?"

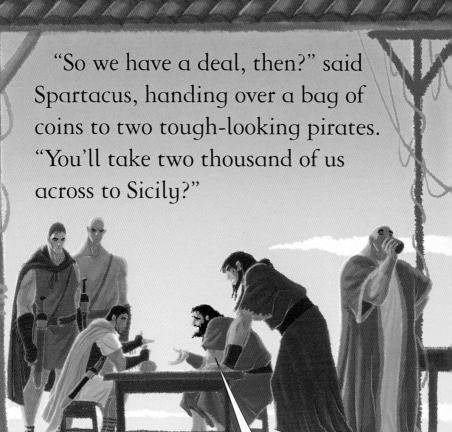

Agreed.

Spartacus knew there had once been a slave rebellion on Sicily. He was sure he could persuade them to rebel once more and join him.

But when Spartacus and his followers arrived at the docks next morning, as arranged, the pirates were nowhere to be seen.

Spartacus felt a fool. "We've been betrayed," he growled. "Now we'll have to head north in search of more men."

It was going to be more difficult than Spartacus could ever imagine.

Chapter 8

The final battle

While Spartacus had been plotting,
Crassus had advanced, trapping his
enemy in the toe of Italy. His men
built a vast barrier across Bruttium,
from the Tyrrhenian Sea to the
Ionian Sea. Spartacus was cut off.

By now, it was winter, 71 B.C.

"We'll wait until spring before we attack," Crassus told his officers. "The rebels will have run out of food. They'll be too weak to stop us."

But the senators in Rome were impatient for victory. Crassus heard they were sending a general named Pompey to finish the job.

Crassus didn't want anyone else stealing his glory. "I'll have to attack now," he decided.

Spartacus knew he had to act too. He took a third of the rebel army and managed to break through Crassus' barrier.

Crassus sent his legions south to fight the rebels left behind. It was an easy victory for the Romans. Spartacus calculated there were now less than 40,000 men left from his once mighty rebel army.

He planned to lead his followers east to Brundisium to escape by sea. But he was frustrated to find it occupied by legions that had just arrived from Macedonia.

Turning back, the rebels wanted one last glorious battle. "Let us have victory or death," they declared.

Spartacus was forced to agree.

A few days later, the slaves came face to face with Crassus and his legions near the River Silarus.

Spartacus led from the front.
The fighting was hard and bloody.
Swords clashed, spears flew in all
directions. The air was filled with
cries of war and screams of death.

The rebel slaves fought bravely.
But it was their last taste of battle.

Crassus had any rebel survivors captured, then executed. In the confusion of the battle, no one saw what finally became of Spartacus. Crassus had his legionaries search the battlefield for his body. But the remains of the infamous rebel leader were never discovered.

Spartacus and the Romans

The city of Rome grew up in Italy around 3,000 years ago. By 264 B.C. the Roman army controlled the whole country and, 400 years later, the Romans were running most of the area around the Mediterranean Sea.

The Romans had a vast workforce of slaves, workers with no rights who were owned by Roman citizens. Most of the slaves were prisoners captured from other countries.

Some slaves, along with deserters from the Roman army like Spartacus, were forced to become gladiators who fought for the Romans' entertainment.

A gladiator
in Thracean
fighting gear.

How we know about Spartacus

Much of Spartacus' life is a mystery. What we do know comes largely from the works of two Greek historians – Plutarch (c.46-120 B.C.) and Appian (c.95-165 B.C.). The story in this book is just one possible version of events.

Glossary

citizen - a free man born in Rome to free Roman parents.

gladiator - a slave or prisoner of war who was trained to fight for public entertainment.

legion - a unit of the Roman army. In 73 B.C., there were about 5,000 soldiers in a legion.

republic - a country or state whose rulers are elected by the people. Rome was a republic from 510 B.C. to 27 B.C.

Senate - the group of men who governed Rome during the republic.

senator - a member of the Senate.

slave - a person with no rights, owned by someone else and used as a worker.

61

Timeline

c.109 B.C. - Spartacus is born in Thrace.

c. 78 B.C. - Spartacus serves as a soldier in the Roman Army.

73 B.C. - Spartacus deserts from the Roman Army.
- Spartacus is captured and sold to Lentulus Batiatus' gladiator school in Capua.
- Spartacus and the rebels escape from the gladiator school and take refuge on Mount Vesuvius. Local troops attack them, but are defeated.
- The rebels are trapped on top of Vesuvius by Claudius Glaber's troops. They escape and make a successful counter attack.
- Another officer is sent from Rome, but is defeated.
- The rebels establish camps across southern Italy.
- Spartacus spends the winter at Thurii.

72 B.C. - Crixus decides to stay in Italy with 3,000 of his men.
- Spartacus marches north to the Apennines.
- Crixus and his men are defeated by Lucius Gellius Publicola. Crixus is killed.

- Spartacus defeats Gnaeus Clodianus and Publicola in a series of battles, culminating at Mutina.
- Some of Spartacus' men cross the Alps to freedom.
- Crassus is sent to defeat Spartacus and the rebels.
- Spartacus and the rebels march to southern Italy.
- The slave army is attacked by Mummius near Ancona. Mummius is defeated. His troops are decimated.
- By winter, Spartacus is forced south to Bruttium by Crassus.
- Spartacus is betrayed by pirates.

71 B.C. - Crassus builds a barrier across the southern tip of Italy.
- Pompey is sent to end the slave revolt.
- Spartacus breaks through Crassus' lines and escapes towards Brundisium. Crassus defeats the rebels left behind.
- Spartacus and his rebels return to confront Crassus' troops near the River Silarus. The rebels are defeated. Spartacus is thought to be dead, though his body is not found.
- 6,000 captured slaves are crucified along the Appian Way as a warning to anyone else who dares to consider rebellion.

A note about dates
The dates referred to in this book are all B.C.
(before the birth of Jesus Christ).

Usborne Quicklinks
For links to websites to find out more about
Spartacus and life in Ancient Rome,
go to the Usborne Quicklinks Website
at **www.usborne.com/quicklinks** and
enter the keyword 'Spartacus'.

Please follow the internet safety guidelines on the
Usborne Quicklinks Website. Usborne Publishing
cannot be responsible for the content of any website
other than its own.

History consultant: Dr. Anne Millard
Series editor: Lesley Sims

First published in 2013 by Usborne Publishing Ltd., Usborne House,
83-85 Saffron Hill, London EC1N 8RT, England. www.usborne.com
Copyright © 2013 Usborne Publishing Ltd.

64